IF FO

MW00884515

Greater Than a Tourist Book Series
Reviews from Readers

I think the series is wonderful and beneficial for tourists to get information before visiting the city.

-Seckin Zumbul, Izmir Turkey

I am a world traveler who has read many trip guides but this one really made a difference for me. I would call it a heartfelt creation of a local guide expert instead of just a guide.

-Susy, Isla Holbox, Mexico

New to the area like me, this is a must have!

 -Joe, Bloomington, USA

This is a good series that gets down to it when looking for things to do at your destination without having to read a novel for just a few ideas.

-Rachel, Monterey, USA

Good information to have to plan my trip to this destination.

-Pennie Farrell, Mexico

Great ideas for a port day.

-Mary Martin USA

Aptly titled, you won't just be a tourist after reading this book. You'll be greater than a tourist!

-Alan Warner, Grand Rapids, USA

Even though I only have three days to spend in San Miguel in an upcoming visit, I will use the author's suggestions to guide some of my time there. An easy read - with chapters named to guide me in directions I want to go.

 -Robert Catapano, USA

Great insights from a local perspective! Useful information and a very good value!

 -Sarah, USA

This series provides an in-depth experience through the eyes of a local. Reading these series will help you to travel the city in with confidence and it'll make your journey a unique one.

-Andrew Teoh, Ipoh, Malaysia

GREATER THAN A TOURIST- DOMINICAN REPUBLIC

50 Travel Tips from a Local

Wanda Compres

Cover designed by: Ivana Stamenkovic
Cover Image: https://pixabay.com/en/las-galeras-samana-2100152/

CZYK Publishing Since 2011.

Greater Than a Tourist
Visit our website at www.GreaterThanaTourist.com

Lock Haven, PA
ISBN: 9781723983443

>TOURIST

50 TRAVEL TIPS FROM A LOCAL

BOOK DESCRIPTION

Are you excited about planning your next trip?

Do you want to try something new?

Would you like some guidance from a local?

If you answered yes to any of these questions, then this Greater Than a Tourist book is for you.

Greater Than a Tourist- Dominican Republic by Wanda Compres offers the inside scoop on Dominican Republic. Most travel books tell you how to travel like a tourist. Although there is nothing wrong with that, as part of the Greater Than a Tourist series, this book will give you travel tips from someone who has lived at your next travel destination.

In these pages, you will discover advice that will help you throughout your stay. This book will not tell you exact addresses or store hours but instead will give you excitement and knowledge from a local that you may not find in other smaller print travel books.

Travel like a local. Slow down, stay in one place, and get to know the people and the culture. By the time you finish this book, you will be eager and prepared to travel to your next destination.

TABLE OF CONTENTS

DEDICATION

This book is dedicated to the great people in my life who always support my love for traveling. To my parents and my sisters, to my lovely husband, and to my son Diego, who at the age of 3 woke up one morning and asked me "where are we going to go today".

Every trip that we have taken together has left an invaluable memory in my heart.

ABOUT THE AUTHOR

Wanda Compres is Dominican writer with a Bachelor in Social Communications – Journalism. Wanda lives in Santiago, Dominican Republic. She loves road trips and exploring new places, she just loves to travel.

Wanda's first writings were in poetry that she published locally and shared with friends in public readings. She currently works as a freelancer translator and journalist.

She was born and raced in the Dominican Republic, in the town of Tamboril, in Santiago. She has lived in different cities around the country and has finally settled back in Santiago, right in the heart of the country.

HOW TO USE THIS BOOK

The Greater Than a Tourist book series was written by someone who has lived in an area for over three months. The goal of this book is to help travelers either dream or experience different locations by providing opinions from a local. The author has made suggestions based on their own experiences. Please do your own research before traveling to the area in case the suggested places are unavailable.

FROM THE PUBLISHER

Traveling can be one of the most important parts of a person's life. The anticipation and memories that you have are some of the best. As a publisher of the Greater Than a Tourist book series, as well as the popular 50 Things to Know book series, we strive to help you learn about new places, spark your imagination, and inspire you. Wherever you are and whatever you do I wish you safe, fun, and inspiring travel.

Lisa Rusczyk Ed. D.
CZYK Publishing

OUR STORY

Traveling is a passion of the "Greater than a Tourist" series creator. Lisa studied abroad in college, and for their honeymoon Lisa and her husband toured Europe. During her travels to Malta, an older man tried to give her some advice based on his own experience living on the island since he was a young boy. She was not sure if she should talk to the stranger but was interested in his advice. When traveling to some places she was wary to talk to locals because she was afraid that they weren't being genuine. Through her travels, Lisa learned how much locals had to share with tourists. Lisa created the "Greater Than a Tourist" book series to help connect people with locals. A topic that locals are very passionate about sharing.

WELCOME TO
> TOURIST

INTRODUCTION

"Twenty years from now you will be more disappointed by the things that you didn't do than by the ones you did do. So throw off the bowlines. Sail away from the safe harbor. Catch the trade winds in your sails. Explore. Dream. Discover."

Mark Twain

Welcome To The Dominican Republic

There are many ways to describe the Dominican Republic but these three words resemble more than anything what this country has to offer: Friendly, Musical and Tropical.

The Dominican culture is very rich in its flavor and rhythm. Expect to hear merengue and bachata everywhere, even when riding in public transportation; and to feel the tasty smell of Dominican seasoning when passing by any house.

13

Shorts and swimsuits are a needed, this is an island, the weather is going to be intense and the beach is at the most an hour away from most cities, and when not, rest assured that there will be a river nearby!

Overall, Dominicans are very talkative and friendly, wear your wider smile and get ready to meet some really nice people.

1. WHERE ARE YOU COMING FROM AND WHERE TO LAND?

We have 11 airports, not all are international though. When flying in you need to consider what your destination will be so that you can better plan what airport to travel through.

If you're heading north (Puerto Plata, Santiago, Constanza, Jarabacoa, Samaná, just to mention some of the most popular destinations) the closest and most common option is a "Cibao International Airport" in Santiago, and "Gregorio Luperón Airport" in Puerto Plata.

"Aeropuerto International Arroyo Barril" in Samaná, is also available, although it is less active and may not have direct flights from every location.

If you are traveling to the east, "Punta Cana International Airport" in Punta Cana, is the busiest airport in the country and the best point of contact when going to cities like: Bavaro, Punta Cana and Cap Cana.

"Aeropuerto Internacional Las Americas", located in Santo Domingo, is the closest international airport when traveling to the south and especially if you are staying in the Capital – Santo Domingo.

2. CUSTOM FEES AT THE AIRPORT

When purchasing a ticket to our country through any airline, it will show a $10.00 dollars entry fee included in the airfare. This used to be paid in cash upon arrival, however this was changed since May 2018.

You will receive a 30-day tourist card at customs and immigration, instead of a visa.

When you departure, all nonresidents need to pay a USD 20.00 departure tax, this could be included in your ticket also, you will need to confirm at the moment of purchase, since not all airlines do.

3. FROM ONE TOWN TO THE NEXT

Public transportation can easily take you from one city to another for a fair price. You can travel using bus services which we call "guaguas". They have fix routes that either take you directly from one end to the other (like from Santo Domingo – east, to Santiago – North) or they could have short stops in some smaller cities in between where you can get off the bus to stretch your legs and buy some snacks. They rarely require switching buses.

The biggest bus companies are Caribe Tours and Metro Tours. They have accessible bus terminals and regular schedules, which helps when planning your trips.

In some cities we also have government managed bus lines that go around the city for about 0.10 cents, they are very comfortable and they have a fix schedule. This, however, is not always very reliable.

Uber is also available in the Dominican Republic, so if you feel more comfortable riding in private cars and keeping track of routes and rides, download the app.

4. BIKING IN THE CITY

The Dominican Republic is yet not suited for cycling, hence biking is not most recommended to be used as a regular mean of transportation.

You will find in your visit that some Dominicans have started to use bicycles to move around, however, Dominican drivers are not exactly accommodating to people on bikes which could result in dangerous situations for you.

Mountain biking here can be very rewarding due to our mountain roads and when riding on lesser used trails. You should consider bringing your own bike thought, we don't have many rental options for this type of bikes.

5. POINTS TO CONSIDER IF YOU RENT A VEHICLE

Most countries drivers' licenses are allowed in the Dominican Republic, you just need to make sure it is valid.

Renting is convenient if you want to get to isolated destinations and also to live the experience of driving in this country.

There are plenty of car rental companies around airport locations and in big cities like Santiago, Santo Domingo and Punta Cana. You will find many familiar agencies to choose from like Hertz, Avis, Alamo and Dollar.

Try to be conservative when driving, be as careful as possible, driving can be a wild experience here.

About gas, most towns have at least one gas station. Gas prices are a bit high in this country.

6. MONEY

The local currency is the Dominican Peso, DOP. You can change international currency at airports and harbors, or simply withdraw pesos form an ATM with your international credit or debit card.

In most cities you can find Banco Popular and Scotiabank which allow withdrawals with Visa and MasterCard. They usually impose a low limit but allow several withdrawals at once.

American Dollars and Euros are sometimes accepted at tourist locations at current exchange rate which is normally visible in a sign or provided by the teller. You can also pay with your international credit or debit card.

You might not be able to change Dominican pesos back at home, so remember to change it before leaving the country.

The average cost of living in this country is fairly low, you can rent an apartment outside the central districts of Santo Domingo for about $250.00 per month. Even lower in other cities.

7. DOMINICAN ROADS

One of the areas where our country still has the most opportunities and needs, is our roads. They can very much go from excellent to awful, sometimes in the same street.

Always be alert, avoid distractions when driving specially at night or when it's raining. You might run into potholes, speed bumps or simply people walking along the roadside.

Some of our roads are very small, which is also a challenge, hence just make sure you are particularly careful and look out for slow moving cars and motorcycles.

If you plan to drive on secondary roads along the coast or in the mountains, is recommended a 4WD.

8. STREET VENDORS

One very common action that may take you by surprise is the street vendors coming up to you with just about anything on sale. Don't be nervous, this is very normal in our country.

You'll experience this when walking on the streets of our bigger cities, so if you're staying at a resort and decide to go for a walk around town you'll must definitely be approached. Also, when driving, traffic lights can be pretty crowded with street vendors.

If you're not interested, don't be afraid to refuse politely and keep walking. But if you are, don't just take their first price. It is ok to haggle!

9. TAKE THE FERRY

There is a ferry line that travels between Mayaguez, in Puerto Rico, and Santo Domingo. The journey takes about 12 hours and it leaves Puerto Rico on Mondays, Wednesdays and Fridays at 8pm, arriving at the Dominican Republic by 8am the next morning.

The ferry line is Ferries del Caribe. The website states that this is a 12 hours ride, however it can be subject to weather conditions. They can have up to three crossings a week, but this is a matter of availability and demand, hence you need to check the website to confirm week's rides.

The price is lower than USD 200.00, it fluctuates in some high demand months, although it is normally steady. Regardless of the price this is definitely the less expensive way to travel from Dominican Republic to Puerto Rico and back.

Our main port is located in Santo Domingo, our capital city, located in the south coast of the country.

10. LET'S HAVE A DRINK

Imported drinks can be found at most restaurants and bars, at least in the bigger cities like Santiago and Santo Domingo. However, you should definitely have one of these three drinks during your visit.

Presidente beers, this is a pilsner beer produced by Cervecería Nacional Dominicana. You can get one at any location where they sell alcoholic drinks. It can have either 5% abv. or 4% -Presidente light. And it comes in three different sizes small 12oz, large 19oz and jumbo 33oz. This beer is very refreshing, so it is customary for Dominicans to have a beer or two at the end of their work day. You might actually see people drinking in the street, this is normal, drinking in the streets is allowed in this country.

Brugal rum, this is actually the name to a variety of rums from the Dominican Republic produced by Brugal & Co. They manufacture anything form low-tier to golden high-end premium. The most known brand is the Brugal Extra Viejo (golden premium). It is ideal to have with coca cola and lemon, this drink is known as Cuba Libre.

Mama Juana, this is a mixture of bark and herbs left to soak in rum, red wine and honey. You can buy this bottles at most local markets and you may even take it with you when leaving, however it will need to be on a checked bag to comply with airline rules and regulations. This drink is known for having healing effects also. It has a strong but sweet taste.

11. WHAT TO EAT

There are three dishes that we Dominicans are best at: Sancocho, Mofongo and the Dominican Flag!

Sancocho is a traditional soup popular in other Latin American countries as well. The Dominican version includes different type of meat (pork, beef and chicken are the most common ones), yucca, plantains, potatoes and some other vegetables. It is normally accompany with rice and avocado.

Mofongo is traditional from Puerto Rico, however it has become very popular and very common in the Dominican Republic for the last decade. It is made with fried, mashed plantains, mixed with pork cracklings (sometimes other meat) and garlic. It is mashed in a wooden pestle to turn it into a tight ball that absorbs the flavors of all other condiments. It is sometimes served directly in the pestle as well, which makes it even more attractive. Something that we added to the recipe is cheese. It is grated cheese is sprinkled on top of it, it is just extremely tasty.

And finally, the Dominican flag. This is our most preferred meal at lunch, is the combination of white rice, beans, meat and green salad (tomato and lettuce).

12. LODGING IN THE DOMINICAN

You'll find plenty of options to suit every pocket and budget in this country. We have from huge, all inclusive, beach resorts to more personal rooms, cabins, and small hostels.

Some common options to find lodging in the different cities of the Dominican Republic are Airbnb, Hostelworld.com and booking.com.

All-inclusive resorts are most popular toward beach cities, while at town cities cabins, small hostels and rooms are the most common.

Hostels are also the best option for backpackers and those looking for more affordable options. You can book a room for about USD 15.00 in pretty much any city, sometimes even less, and in most cases breakfast is included.

13. USING MAPS

You can use your phone's GPS and Google Guide to get around easily if you have internet on it. Wi-Fi is not available everywhere, but at most urban areas and especially around malls, bars and restaurants you'll get free access.

Other options to consider could be buying a city or town map, like Mapas GAAR in Santo Domingo; or National Geographic Adventure Map, these are both pretty recommended options.

If you get lost, don't be afraid to ask the locals. Dominicans are very friendly and enjoy helping others, we take pride on guiding others. But be ready to hear some really creative instructions. A big part of our population still doesn't have access to greater education, this can be noticed in the way we talk, our vocabulary can be very enlightening.

14. MERENGUE

Our country is most known for our popular musical style called merengue. This is a lively, fast paced rhythm and dance music. The instruments used are primarily drums, chorded instruments, a güira and an accordion. This rhythm is considered the national dance of our country.

There is a story of the origins of merengue that alleges that it originated when slaves were chained together it forced them to drag one leg as they cut sugar to the beat of drums. And from there the dance style where the ladies follows the steps of the male.

There are three types of merengue, perico ripiao-or merengue tipico (classic, fast paced), Orquesta Merengue and Guitar Merengue (slower paced)

Merengue is very popular out of the country as well, and on your next visit you will listen to it everywhere. The next cool thing is that it is actually very easy to learn too, if you are staying at a resort they normally offer classes for free as part of their daily attractions.

There is a popular Merengue Festival every year, since 1967, in Santo Domingo where Dominican and international merengue bands perform all night.

15. THE WEATHER

The weather in this country is tropical, it is mostly sunny and nice all the time, however we get unexpected climate changes even over really short distances. But unless there is going to be a storm, you don't have to worry too much.

The average temperature is between 25 and 28 degrees Celsius. At higher mountains low temperatures of 0 degrees are possible, especially between January and February, our coolest months.

August is the hottest month here but even then, temperatures are not that high. However between August and October we have tropical cyclones season, don't forget to check the weather forecast before you book any outdoor activities within those months.

16. ELECTRICITY

Electricity can be somewhat unreliable in this country. Although this is an area where the country has experience substantial growth, we still struggle with occasional blackouts, but mostly in residential areas.

Tourist areas tend to have more reliable power, and so do business, travel, healthcare and vital infrastructure.

The electricity voltage in the Dominican Republic is 110 volts, 60 Hz. If your country is in the range of 220-240V I would suggest having a voltage converter to protect your devices. You can buy voltage converters in Amazon.

A good way to be sure is to check the label on your appliances, that way you can get ready before packing.

17. LANGUAGE

Here in the Dominican Republic we speak Spanish as our native language. Our language is very rich in regionalism and words borrowed from other languages, so don't feel embarrassed if you don't understand much of what we say on your first interactions, this will be a funny story to bring back home!

Tourism, American pop culture and the influence of Dominican Americans have had a great impact on our language, hence it is not rare to find English speakers almost everywhere.

Other popular languages spoken by Dominicans are Italian, German and French. Especially at tourist sites they always make sure to have these languages available for visitors. Even more, when you stay at an all-inclusive resort, you'll find that all announcements are made in different languages.

18. VISUAL ARTS

This country has a long history of fine arts, we have abundant historical sites, museums and colonial architecture. At the capital, Santo Domingo, you'll find 10 museums with exhibits ranging from semiprecious gems to prehistoric art.

If you are into being amazed by Dominican history visit The Museum of the Dominican Man with traces of our origin back to the Tainos. Other museums include The National Museum of Natural History, Museum of the Dominican Family, National Museum of History and Geography, and the Museum of Modern Art.

And for theater enthusiast we have the National Theater, also in Santo Domingo, which features theatrical, musical and dance performances; along with cultural events and exhibits in its garden.

There is also a theater in Santiago called "El Gran Teatro del Cibao". This is the second biggest scenario in the country. It holds up to 1,678 guests.

Tickets for both theaters can be bought at the entrance or purchased online at their website. Prices depend on the show being presented. The dress code for any event in this theaters is formal.

19. BASEBALL SEASON

Baseball is big in this country. We love our sport and our teams. We have the second highest number of baseball players in the MLB.

We have six baseball clubs that represent different regions, but the most intense rivalry is Licey, from Santo Domingo, and Aguilas Cibaeñas, from Santiago. A trip to the Estadio Quisqueya Juan Marichal, in Santo Domingo or Estadio Cibao in Santiago to watch those two contenders can be very exhilarating.

At these ball parks, tickets can be bought upon arrival or ahead of the game, this could be the best option since some of these games can be sold out fairly quickly.

The Estadio Quisqueya has 11,379 seats. It was built in 1955 and it was renamed after the former Major League Baseball player and Hall of famer Juan Marichal.

The Estadio Cibao's capacity is 18,077 seats, it is the largest in the country. It was built in 1958. It has an extended visitors' club house, multi-use stage behind home field and a museum of The Aguilas Cibaeñas history.

20. STAY HYDRATED

The weather here is hot, and most likely your time here is going to be very active and include plenty of drinks. So you need to make sure that you hydrate.

Some visitors have experienced some stomach discomfort when drinking water directly for fountains, so it is probably best to drink from sealed water bottles. Lockley water is very inexpensive here.

This country is also home to many tropical fruits, especially coconuts. It is very common to find people selling coconuts on the street side where you can buy only the water or the entire fruit.

This is a very nutritious drink. When you buy some, look for young coconuts as they have a sweeter taste than older ones.

21. ETHNIC GROUPS

Most of our population (73%) is of racially mixed origin. Ethnic immigrant groups here include west and East Asian and Europeans.

In the past century we've experienced the immigration of many Arabs, Japanese and Koreans as agricultural laborers and merchants.

We are descendants of black African slaves and white Europeans, our race is known as mulatos or mestizos, which is how most Dominicans identify themselves.

Since 2017 we have been receiving a really high volume of Venezuelan immigrants driven by the economic and political crisis they have experienced. This immigrants have been joining the workforce fairly actively.

22. CHARGING YOUR DEVICES

Here we use a two-flat-pins electricity plugs, similar to the US, if you have a two-round-pins plug you will need to buy an adapter.

If you're staying at an all-inclusive hotel they might be able to provide you with on during your stay or will probably have some for sale at their local shops. You should ask at the hotel's reception.

There are many places you can buy an adapter for your devices. We have some department stores that have a shop at almost every big city in the country, you can google them, here are some names: La Sirena, Plaza Lama and Jumbo.

23. PICK YOUR TERRAIN – MOUNTAINS

One of the great things about this island is that you can find different types of landform without having to travel too far.

Looking for mountain scenery? Come to center of the country, towards the North. From the city of La Vega you get access to Jarabacoa and Constanza. These two mountain country cities have spectacular views of the forest and lower temperatures than the rest of the country.

Flowers and ornamental plants are gown in this cities, hence there are multiple street markets and gardens. When staying at one of the local small hostels you will wake up to the splendid smell of pine trees, flowers and fruits.

During the months of January, February and March the temperature here can reach -5 degrees.

24. SMELLS LIKE SALT AND SUN!

The Dominican Republic is famous for its white sand beaches with coconut trees enhancing the already marvelous view.

Over the weekend it is very common for Dominican families to drive to the beach, so they are normally very crowded, there is music and plenty of food. There are also bars and restaurants on most Dominican beaches.

Beaches facing the Caribbean are usually safe year round, however those on the northern coastline require attention to the forecast before going into the water.

Some of the most popular and beautiful beach destinations to visit are Punta Cana, Samana, Puerto Plata and Bahía de Las Aguilas. This last one is on the south of the country and it will definitely leave you speechless.

25. LOS HAITISES NATIONAL PARK

Los Haitises National Park is a protected virgin forest. It has little road access and the number of tourists allowed is limited. You'll need an ecological guide to access it.

This park has the greatest diversity of fauna in the country including some endemic species. The weather is very humid, there are many species of orchids and other Caribbean flowers. And let's not forget the caverns with pictograms and petroglyphs, and the mangroves along its bay.

It is located in Sabana de la Mar, province of Hato Mayor, which is where the site of visitors center is located.

26. CLIMB THE PICO DUARTE

If you're a nature and hiking lover being able to reach the top of Pico Duarte, the highest mountain in the Dominican Republic and the Caribbean, will give you a sense of pride.

Located in the Jose Armando Bermudez National Park, Pico Duarte is over 3,000 meters (10,000+ feet) high. There are at least 5 hiking routes, the most popular one is "La Cienaga" which usually takes 3 days and 23.1 kilometers of hiking, it's the shortest and easiest way up.

This is a wonderful adventure that requires preparation, here are some tips to consider: wear hiking boots, wool socks, pack light, bring water thermos and a tarp - the weather is unpredictable, and bring a warm blanket, it can get pretty cold.

You'll need a guide to go into this park, it can be very dangerous if you try to make it on your own. You can get a local tour guide at the entrance, but my recommendation is to book with a tour organizer, they'll have it all figure out and you won't have to worry about every detail.

27. TRAMWAYS – PUERTO PLATA CABLE CAR

One fun thing to do in the Dominican Republic is riding on the cable car in Puerto Plata.

This is located on the "Isabel de Torres" mountain, and at the top of the ride there is a fortress with a statue of the "Crist the Redeemer" with open arms as if welcoming visitors.

This attraction is open from 8am to 5pm. There is also a snack bar at the top where you can sit and enjoy an outstanding view of the mountains on your back and the beach up front.

This is best enjoyed on sunny days, no reservation needed. You can simply buy your ticket upon arrival. And you can leave your vehicle parked at the entrance, take the ride up, enjoy some time at the fortress, explore the flora, and return to starting point!

28. "27 CHARCOS" – THE 27 WATERFALLS

When on your way to Puerto Plata plan a stop at the city of Damajagua for an exciting adventure at the 27 Waterfalls.

This experience includes walking through waterfall trails and ponds, jumping into the river and exploring nature at its best. It takes about two to three hours to make it to the top and back, or you could opt to walk only to the 7th waterfall of this hidden treasure if you want the short version.

You get there and walk with a local guide, which are available at the entrance, or you can book a tour from Puerto Plata with an ecotourism agency which normally includes transportation on a safari monster truck, drinks, a meal, safety garment, and a tour guide. This tour could take up to 9 hours since they generally take you to other typical or cultural places too.

If you're bringing your kids, they need to be over 11 years old to be allowed on the hike and, what's most important, bring strong, hiking and water resistant shoes.

29. CARE FOR A CIGAR?

If you are one to enjoy a good cigar then Santiago, directly south of Puerto Plata needs to be in your travel plan. This city is home to Dominican Republic's finest and biggest tobacco and cigar industries.

La Aurora Cigar Factory offers a day trip around their Premium cigar factory, it lasts less than an hour and it introduces you to the process of making a cigars and the history of La Aurora. They have a cigar museum as well. You can book this tour from TripAdvisor or directly with the Factory.

If you are thinking more like enjoying a good smoke, you'll find many cigar bars where you can sit in comfortable chairs (or rocking chairs), buy your preferred cigar and a drink to go with it.

The brands manufactured here are well known around the world.

30. PUT ON A MASK, IT'S CARNIVAL TIME

Between the months of February and March, main streets of the Dominican Republic's biggest cities are found to be full of color, music and festive parades. It is carnival time!

The carnival is a really big event in this country. It goes on all over the country but there are two cities that have the biggest celebrations: Santo Domingo and La Vega.

Traditional customs are mostly "Diablos" (devils), these are much elaborated outfits with bright colors, plenty of sequins and impressive masks. They sometimes carry either a balloon or a whip which they use to perform "fights" between each other or with other groups.

Bring your camera so that you can capture these colorful scenery, however, keep in mind that these parades are very crowded, and so be aware of your belongings at all times.

31. WATER RAFTING AND TUBING

The high altitude of some of our mountains makes the Dominican Republic ideal for rafting experiences. The water of the Yaque del Norte River – longest in the Caribbean, has the sufficient force from high summits to make this an unforgettable experience.

This is available all year long at the city of Jarabacoa, although both rafting and tubing are most popular during summer months when water levels are sufficiently high.

You can find great places and deals to live this experience in TripAdvisor. Places that offer this experience normally also include all garment required.

32. HUMPBACK WHALES SANCTUARY

Located in Samana, an only available from December to March every year, this is one of the most beautiful experiences ever.

About 2,000 humpback whales come to reproduce in the warm waters of the Atlantic Ocean every year, it is an amazing sight. You get to see the 40-ton males jump up the water and fall down a few meters ahead.

Samana is consider one of the best places in the world for humpback whales watching. This is normally a full day tour which includes a visit to the sanctuary in safe boats, lunch and drinks.

33. COLONIA DISTRICT

The Colonial District, in Santo Domingo, most known as "Zona Colonial" is the oldest city in the Americas. Is a trip to the time of Columbus with a XXI century touch. It has a high number of landmarks and is one of the main tourist attractions in Santo Domingo, with a lot of commercial activity, bars, restaurants and many prominent landmarks.

Some of the places to visit should include: Alcazar de Colon (oldest Viceregal residence in the Americas), Catedral de Santa María la Menor (oldest cathedral), La Puerta del Conde (where the Dominican Independence was proclaimed in 1844), Museo de Las Casa Reales, and Calle del Conde where you can have an outdoor meal or drinks.

You can walk to the different places since everything if fairly close, take the Chu-Chu train in

Calle Isabel La Católica, or rent a bike and ride around.

34. THE NATIONAL BOTANICAL GARDEN

This park was named after a Dominican botanist who cataloged a big range of plants in the country, its official name is The Dr. Rafael M. Moscoso Botanical Garden.

This park has some remarkable endemism birds and vegetation, it features collections of bromeliads, ferns, palms, medicinal plants and over 300 type of orchids.

It is a popular destination for bird watchers and it also has a traditional Japanese garden!

The park's symbol is the leave of a guanito (a common palm tree) and it can be found in various representations in the garden.

If you don't want to walk too much, there is a chu-chu train that takes you on a guided tour.

35. VISIT THE ALCAZAR DE COLON AT NIGHT

This historic structure was built in the 1510' and was restored later on. It is a Spanish castle built for Christopher Columbus and his family, and is a monument to Spanish rule during the sixteenth century. It was one of the oldest remaining buildings in the Americas.

It's especially breathtaking at night, it has lots of restaurants overlooking the square and plenty of security personnel so you don't need to be concerned about safety when the sun goes down.

The Alcazar is a fun historical landmark to visit, they charge a very minimal fee to get in and guides are available to provide you with insights.

36. FINE DINING

Part of experiencing a foreign culture need to include eating at least one expensive meal. And here even the finest restaurants are semi casual.

A very well-known restaurant in Punta Cana is "Bachata Rosa", this restaurant is owned by a renowned Dominican artist – Juan Luis Guerra.

Some really fine restaurants can be found at resorts and hotel restaurants, they take the local cousin to a gourmet level. Other strongly recommended options include: "La Yola", at the Punta Cana Resort and Club; "Passion", at the Paradisus Palma Real – also in Punta Cana; and "El Meson de Cava", in a natural limestone cavern in Santo Domingo.

37. DOMINICAN FLAVORS

One way to try some of Dominican's must popular flavors is booking a Rum, Tobacco and Chocolate tour. This can be a very cultural excursion where you'll get to know the flavor and aroma of our most famous products.

This tour is available at Altos de Chavon, in La Romana.

They'll take you into a Tabacalera where you'll see handmade cigars in process and then to the Cigar Museum Country Megastore. The tour continues to the Chocolate Museum to discover the secrets of how cocoa is used. And to conclude this experience, there is a visit to the famous rum factory of Barceló, a brand founded in 1930. And of course, they'll be a rum tasting!

38. CAVES AND CAVERNS

Caves and caverns were significant to our ancestors, the Tainos, they used to live in them and there is a great deal of cultural and spiritual history on their walls.

There are caves in different cities of the country, some of the ones I most recommend visiting are these ones: Cueva de Las Maravillas (La Romana) This cave has been awarded the 2003 Gold Prize in the International Landscape Architecture Bienal Award. Paths and lightning have been install to make the journey even more remarkable.

"Los Tres Ojos", this is a National Park right in the middle of Santo Domingo. You pay an entrance fee, no guide required –they are available though, and you can walk through the trails and explore three magnificent caves at once. There is a picnic area and a cafeteria inside the park as well.

39. ISLA SAONA

This beautiful island is located at short distance of the DR. on the south-east of Bayahibe. It is a very popular tourist destination for its white sand and turquoise water, so beautiful that it has been used on international films and advertisements.

It is a government protected nature reserve, part of the Nacional Park Cotubanama. You get there in a catamaran or a small motorboat.

The Saona Island is the most important turtle nesting side in the country. It is also considered a bird heaven and tons of starfish can be found in a Natural Pool.

Bring your camera if you're looking for more than just hanging out at the beach, however, remember that this is a protected park and you need to respect this islands resource, so don't touch the wild life!

40. SAFARI EXPERIENCE

Many different safaris are offered in Dominican Tourist and Travel agencies which ranged from jeeps, 4-wheels, super trucks, sea buggies, and others.

This safaris sometimes go on the roads and visit different towns, or go specifically into nature and drive through rough roads. Either way they are very exciting.

Colonial Tours is the travel agency where I've seen more options and they have tours all over the country. On some of their safaris they even take you to a typical Dominican house in the country where they do fruit tasting and watch cockfights.

41. WHEN THINKING ABOUT THE SOUTH – THINK BARAHONA

A visit to the deep southwest of the Dominican Republic is an adventure that you should definitely consider if you are a fan of remoteness.

Reserves and national parks, surfing beaches and fresh water cascades give this town the nickname "Pearl of the South".

Here are some of the destinations that you should include in your itinerary: Sierra de Bahoruco National Park, a dry forest with unique endemic species and rhinoceros iguanas; local artisan marmalade making session at Cooperativa La Cienaga – this is delicious; Chase after gemstones at the Larimar Mine or at the Escuela, Taller y Museo de Larimar, you can get very affordable artisan gifts for friends and family here.

42. TAKE A DIP AT HOYO AZUL

As impressive as it can be, swimming at this 65-meter high cliff is open to visitors, so plan to dip into it turquois water.

It is located just a short hike into the woods in Punta Cana.

It is open between 9am and 3pm, and an entrance fee is required. Devices like cameras, drones or even phones are not allowed at the dip.

It takes a good walk to get there, so remember to wear sunscreen, comfortable clothing, and strong shoes.

43. DISCO AT PUNTA CANA

They say you can party anywhere, and in the Dominican Republic this is more than true, we are a very festive culture. However, if you want to enjoy a spectacular night and have an experience that you will never forget, you need to go to Coco Bongo downtown in Punta Cana.

Incredible live shows cinema, theater, musicals, disco, videos, acrobatics, technology, actors, public, surprises. Coco Bongo is strategically located in a centralized area of Bavaro, city of Veron, in Punta

Cana near most hotels, amenities and the local Punta Cana International Airport.

This three levels nightclub is characterized by an impeccable display of lights and sound.

44. MUSICAL FESTIVALS

This country is very musical, you could easily catch concerts or festivals year round in different scenarios. We have the most fascinating arrays of annual festivals in Latin America.

If you like instrumental and classical music, the Sinfonica Nacional concerts season is held between the months of August and October at the National Theater in Santo Domingo. They have other concerts at different locations around the country, you will need to check their itinerary to confirm.

For a more popular experience, we have the Verano Presidente. This is a three days music festival held yearly and sponsored primarily by Presidente beer. It presents different artists (national and international) and of different genres as well. This festival is held in September.

Festival de Merengue happens between July and August and is one of the best ways to fully understand the Dominican culture. It is conducted at the Malecon, in Santo Domingo, and music simply goes on all night.

45. GOLF

If you enjoy golfing you'll be pleased to learn that the Dominican Republic has one of the most magnificent golf courses in the Caribbean and Latin America.

At least 7 Dominican courses have topped Golf Week Magazine's Top 50. So where to go?

We have courses in Punta Cana, Juan Dolio (at Santo Domingo), La Romana and Puerto Plata. Since these are all tourist destinations you will most definitely find English speaking personnel.

The "Teeth of the Dog", at Casa de Campo, is the number one spot since 2009.

46. BUYING SOUVENIRS

The first recommendation about souvenirs is not to buy them from Tourist stores, but buy them at local markets. Not only because of the inflated prices but also to support the locals.

Some great gifts to bring back home with you include: Amber or Larimer jewels, coconut artiness, Mamajuana, Dominican Rum, or a miniature Dominican instrument like a güira or a drum.

If you want to bring a memoir of these unforgettable holidays you can also buy some Taino crafts and figures produced in clay. They make a very peculiar and attractive addition to your decoration.

Some people also buy Dominican's coffee or chocolate to prologue the taste of our culture in their palade. You can buy intense or light grain, but it will always have that unique aroma that will remind you of your days in this country.

47. VOLUNTEERING IN THE DOMINICAN REPUBLIC

There are many volunteering opportunities in the Dominican Republic, some organizations offer extended travel for people willing to work with locals on projects such as community development, conservation, wildlife sanctuary maintenance and scientific research.

Some of the volunteer programs in place in the Dominican Republic are Dream.org, which has both a summer camp and a yearlong program; FRONTIER, most placements are organized in groups and are available year round. Some organizations charge a sign-up fee, this would need to be confirmed on the program's website.

These programs are open to all nationalities and normally require you to be aged 18+. Some happen in Santo Domingo and/or Santiago, however others take place in more rural areas.

48. SENSITIVE TOPICS

As any other country there are some topics that is best to avoid when visiting to prevent unnecessary confrontation that may get in the way of your enjoyment and compromise lasting connections.

Politics, like everywhere else, is one of them. Although, we like to talk about politics and we are very vocal about our opinions, this topic is a well-known sensitive area for every country.

We share the island with the country of Haiti, from which we have a strained over mass Haitian migration. Some people have their own opinion and feel very strong about this, so my recommendation is to avoid commenting on the Dominican-Haitian confrontation.

49. UNIQUE STONES

We have two endemic stones here in the Dominican Republic Amber and Larimar.

Amber is the result of warm climate and the extinct prehistoric leguminous tree, Humenaea Protera. It is consider the finest in the word because of the high concentration of fossils included

Larimar is a rare blue variation of silicate mineral pectolite, its color varies form light blue, to green blue, to deep blue. It is said that Larimar stimulates the heart, throat, third eye and crown chakras facilitating inner wisdom to outer manifestation.

They are both used to create very original accessories (earrings, necklaces and even rings) which are sold at impressively low prices. They can be purchased at local markets or at any tourist shop.

50. WHEN TO TIP

It is common and, is most cases, expected to provide tips to Dominican servers. Guests can leave tips either in pesos on in their local currency. The value of the DOP is usually around 45 to 50 US dollars.

Guests normally leave a small tip for maids when staying at hotels, or provide at tip upon their exit to guest services and amenities personal. Resort's gratuity policy is generally available when booking a vacation and, although it might be included in your rate, it is just a nice thing to do. After all, this employees work really long hours and get paid low rates.

Also, at service locations like beauty and nail salons, spas, to drivers, bellboys, restaurants and bars it is customary to leave a tip.

At restaurant and bars a 10% gratuity is the usual if you've enjoyed the service, it can sometimes be added to your bill, so you should always check you tab before leaving extras, now if your service was beyond good, you can also give an additional tip straight to your waiter or waitress.

TOP REASONS TO BOOK THIS TRIP

The Dominican Culture is very rich, you'll find landmarks, old structures and history on every corner.

There are only a few beaches in the word that can compare to those here. White sand beauty and the perfect weather to enjoy it.

Here you can find different vacation options, from quiet and relaxing, to fun and exhilarating experiences.

BONUS BOOK

50 THINGS TO KNOW ABOUT PACKING LIGHT FOR TRAVEL

PACK THE RIGHT WAY EVERY TIME

AUTHOR: MANIDIPA BHATTACHARYYA

Edited by Melanie Howthorne

ABOUT THE AUTHOR

Manidipa Bhattacharyya is a creative writer and editor, with an education in English literature and Linguistics. After working in the IT industry for seven long years she decided to call it quits and follow her heart instead. Manidipa has been ghost writing, editing, proof reading and doing secondary research services for many story tellers and article writers for about three years. She stays in Kolkata, India with her husband and a busy two year old. In her own time Manidipa enjoys travelling, photography and writing flash fiction.

Manidipa believes in travelling light and never carries anything that she couldn't haul herself on a trip. However, travelling with her child changed the scenario. She seemed to carry the entire world with her for the baby on the first two trips. But good sense prevailed and she is again working her way to becoming a light traveler, this time with a kid.

INTRODUCTION

*He who would travel happily
must travel light.*

-Antoine de Saint-Exupéry

Travel takes you to different places from seas and mountains to deserts and much more. In your travels you get to interact with different people and their cultures. You will, however, enjoy the sights and interact positively with these new people even more, if you are travelling light.

When you travel light your mind can be free from worry about your belongings. You do not have to spend precious vacation time waiting for your luggage to arrive after a long flight. There is be no chance of your bags going missing and the best part is that you need not pay a fee for checked baggage.

People who have mastered this art of packing light will root for you to take only one carry-on, wherever you go. However, many people can find it really hard to pack light. More so if you are travelling with children. Differentiating between "must have" and "just in case" items is the starting point. There will be ample shopping avenues at your destination which are just waiting to be explored.

This book will show you 'packing' in a new 'light' –
pun intended – and help you to embrace light
packing practices for all of your future travels.

Off to packing!

DEDICATION

I dedicate this book to all the travel buffs that I know,
who have given me great insights into the contents of
their backpacks.

THE RIGHT TRAVEL GEAR

1. CHOOSE YOUR TRAVEL GEAR CAREFULLY

While selecting your travel gear, pick items that are
light weight, durable and most importantly, easy to
carry. There are cases with wheels so you can drag
them along – these are usually on the heavy side
because of the trolley. Alternatively a backpack that
you can carry comfortably on your back, or even a
duffel bag that you can carry easily by hand or sling
across your body are also great options. Whatever
you choose, one thing to keep in mind is that the
luggage itself should not weigh a ton, this will give
you the flexibility to bring along one extra pair of
shoes if you so desire.

2. CARRY THE MINIMUM NUMBER OF BAGS

Selecting light weight luggage is not everything. You need to restrict the number of bags you carry as well. One carry-on size bag is ideal for light travel. Most carriers allow one cabin baggage plus one purse, handbag or camera bag as long as it slides under the seat in front. So technically, you can carry two items of luggage without checking them in.

3. PACK ONE EXTRA BAG

Always pack one extra empty bag along with your essential items. This could be a very light weight duffel bag or even a sturdy tote bag which takes up minimal space. In the event that you end up buying a lot of souvenirs, you already have a handy bag to stuff all that into and do not have to spend time hunting for an appropriate bag.

I'm very strict with my packing and have everything in its right place. I never change a rule. I hardly use anything in the hotel room. I wheel my own wardrobe in and that's it.

Charlie Watts

CLOTHES & ACCESSORIES

4. PLAN AHEAD

Figure out in advance what you plan to do on your trip. That will help you to pick that one dress you need for the occasion. If you are going to attend a wedding then you have to carry formal wear. If not, you can ditch the gown for something lighter that will be comfortable during long walks or on the beach.

5. WEAR THAT JACKET

Remember that wearing items will not add extra luggage for your air travel. So wear that bulky jacket that you plan to carry for your trip. This saves space and can also help keep you warm during the chilly flight.

6. MIX AND MATCH

Carry clothes that can be interchangeably used to reinvent your look. Find one top that goes well with a couple of pairs of pants or skirts. Use tops, shirts and jackets wisely along with other accessories like a scarf or a stole to create a new look.

7. CHOOSE YOUR FABRIC WISELY

Stuffing clothes in cramped bags definitely takes its toll which results in wrinkles. It is best to carry wrinkle free, synthetic clothes or merino tops. This will eliminate the need for that small iron you usually bring along.

8. DITCH CLOTHES PACK UNDERWEAR

Pack more underwear and socks. These are the things that will give you a fresh feel even if you do not get a chance to wear fresh clothes. Moreover these are easy to wash and can be dried inside the hotel room itself.

9. CHOOSE DARK OVER LIGHT

While picking your clothes choose dark coloured ones. They are easy to colour coordinate and can last longer before needing a wash. Accidental food spills and dirt from the road are less visible on darker clothes.

10. WEAR YOUR JEANS

Take only one pair of Jeans with you, which you should wear on the flight. Remember to pick a pair that can be worn for sightseeing trips and is equally eloquent for dinner. You can add variety by adding light weight cargoes and chinos.

11. CARRY SMART ACCESSORIES

The right accessory can give you a fresh look even with the same old dress. An intelligent neck-piece, a couple of bright scarves, stoles or a sarong can be used in a number of ways to add variety to your clothing. These light weight beauties can double up as a nursing cover, a light blanket, beach wear, a modesty cover for visiting places of worship, and also makes for an enthralling game of peek-a-boo.

12. LEARN TO FOLD YOUR GARMENTS

Seasoned travellers all swear by rolling their clothes for compact and wrinkle free packing. Bundle packing, where you roll the clothes around a central object as if tying it up, is also a popular method of compact and wrinkle free packing. Stacking folded clothes one on top of another is a big no-no as it makes creases extreme and they are difficult to get rid of without ironing.

13. WASH YOUR DIRTY LAUNDRY

One of the ways to avoid carrying loads of clothes is to wash the clothes you carry. At some places you might get to use the laundry services or a Laundromat but if you are in a pinch, best solution is to wash them yourself. If that is the plan then carrying quick drying clothes is highly recommended, which most often also happen to be the wrinkle free variety.

14. LEAVE THOSE TOWELS BEHIND

Regular towels take up a lot of space, are heavy and take ages to dry out. If you are staying at hotels they will provide you with towels anyway. If you are travelling to a remote place, where the availability of towels look doubtful, carry a light weight travel towel of viscose material to do the job.

15. USE A COMPRESSION BAG

Compression bags are getting lots of recommendation now days from regular travellers. These are useful for saving space in your luggage when you have to pack bulky dresses. While packing for the return trip, get help from the hotel staff to arrange a vacuum cleaner.

FOOTWEAR

16. PUT ON YOUR HIKING BOOTS

If you have plans to go hiking or trekking during your trip, you will need those bulky hiking boots. The best way to carry them is to wear them on flight to save space and luggage weight. You can remove the boots once inside and be comfortable in your socks.

17. PICKING THE RIGHT SHOES

Shoes are often the bulkiest items, along with being the dainty if you are a female. They need care and take up a lot of space in your luggage. It is advisable therefore to pick shoes very carefully. If you plan to do a lot of walking and site seeing, then wearing a pair of comfortable walking shoes are a must. For more formal occasions you can carry durable, light weight flats which will not take up much space.

18. STUFF SHOES

If you happen to pack a pair of shoes, ensure you utilize their hollow insides. Tuck small items like rolled up socks or belts to save space. They will also be easy to find.

TOILETRIES

19. STASHING TOILETRIES

Carry only absolute necessities. Airline rules dictate that for one carry-on bag, liquids and gels must be in 3.4 ounce (100ml) bottles or less, and must be packed in a one quart zip-lock bag. If you are planning to stay in a hotel, the basic things will be provided for you. It's best is to buy the rest from the local market at your destination.

20. TAKE ALONG TAMPONS

Tampons are a hard to find item in a lot of countries. Figure out how many you need and pack accordingly. For longer stays you can buy them online and have them delivered to where you are staying.

21. GET PAMPERED BEFORE YOU TRAVEL

Some avid travellers suggest getting a pedicure and manicure just the day before travelling. This not only gives you a well kept look, you also save the trouble of packing nail polish. Remember, every little bit of weight reduced adds up.

ELECTRONICS

22. LUGGING ALONG ELECTRONICS

Electronics have a large role to play in our lives today. Most of us cannot imagine our lives away from our phones, laptops or tablets. However while travelling, one must consider the amount of weight these electronics add to our luggage. Thankfully smart phones come along with all the essentials tools like a camera, email access, picture editing tools and more. They are smart to the point of eliminating the need to carry multiple gadgets. Choose a smart phone that suits all your requirements and travel with the world in your palms or pocket.

23. REDUCE THE NUMBER OF CHARGERS

If you do travel with multiple electronic devices, you will have to bear the additional burden of carrying all their chargers too. Check if a single charger can be used for multiple devices. You might also consider investing in a pocket charger. These small devices support multiple devices while keeping you charged on the go.

24. TRAVEL FRIENDLY APPS

Along with smart phones come numerous apps, which are immensely helpful in our travels. You name it and you have an app for it at hand – take pictures, sharing with friends and family, torch to light dark roads, maps, checking flight/train times, find hotels and many other things. Use these smart alternatives to traditional items like books to eliminate weight and save space.

I get ideas about what's essential when packing my suitcase.

-Diane von Furstenberg

TRAVELLING WITH KIDS

25. BRING ALONG THE STROLLER

Kids might enjoy walking for a while but they soon tire out and a stroller is the just the right thing for them to rest in while you continue your tour. Strollers also double duty as a luggage carrier and shopping bag holder. Remember to pick a light weight, easy to handle brand of stroller. Better yet, find out in advance if you can rent a stroller at your destination.

26. BRING ONLY ENOUGH DIAPERS FOR YOUR TRIP

Diapers take up a lot of space and add to the weight of your luggage. Therefore it is advisable to carry just enough diapers to last through the trip and a few for afterwards, till you buy fresh stock at your destination. Unless of course you are travelling to a really remote area, in which case you have no choice but to carry the load. Otherwise diapers are something you will find pretty easily.

27. TAKE ONLY A COUPLE OF TOYS

Children are easily attracted by new things in their environment. While travelling they will find numerous 'new' objects to scrutinize and play with. Packing just one favorite toy is enough, or if there is no favorite toy leave out all of them in favor of stories or imaginary games.

28. CARRY KID FRIENDLY SNACKS

Create a small snack counter in your bag to store away quick bites for those sudden hunger pangs. Depending on the child's age this could include chocolates, raisins, dry fruits, granola bars or biscuits. Also keep a bottle of water handy for your little one.

These things do not add much weight and can be adjusted in a handbag or knapsack.

29. GAMES TO CARRY

Create some travel specific, imaginary games if you have slightly grown up children, like spot the attractions. Keep a coloring book and colors handy for in-flight or hotel time. Apps on your smart phone can keep the children engaged with cartoons and story books. Older children are often entertained by games available on phones or tablets. This cuts the weight of luggage down while keeping the kids entertained.

30. LET THE KIDS CARRY THEIR LOAD

A good thing is to start early sharing of responsibilities. Let your child pick a bag of his or her choice and pack it themselves. Keep tabs on what they are stuffing in their bags by asking if they will be using that item on the trip. It could start out being just an entertainment bag initially but with growing years they will learn to sort the useful from the superfluous. Children as little as four can maneuver a small trolley suitcase like a pro- their experience in pull along toys credit. If you are worried that you may be pulling it for them, you may want to start with a backpack.

31. DECIDE ON LOCATION FOR CHILDREN TO SLEEP

While on a trip you might not always get a crib at your destination, and carrying one will make life all the more difficult. Instead call ahead to see if there are any cribs or roll out beds for children. You may even put blankets on the floor. Weave them a story about camping and they will gladly sleep without any trouble.

32. GET BABY PRODUCTS DELIVERED AT YOUR DESTINATION

If you are absolutely paranoid about not getting your favourite variety of diaper or brand of baby food, check out online stores like amazon.com for services in your destination city. You can buy things online ahead of your travel and get them delivered to your hotel upon arrival.

33. FEEDING NEEDS OF YOUR INFANTS

If you are travelling with a breastfed infant, you save the trouble of carrying bottles and bottle sanitization kits. For special food, or medications, you may need

to call ahead to make sure you have a refrigerator
where you are staying.

34. FEEDING NEEDS OF YOUR TODDLER

With the progression from infancy to toddler, their
dietary requirements too evolve. You will have to
pack some snacks for travelling time. Fresh fruits and
vegetables can be purchased at your destination. Most
of the cities you travel to in whichever part of the
world, will have baby food products and formulas,
available at the local drug-store or the supermarket.

35. PICKING CLOTHES FOR YOUR BABY

Contrary to popular belief, babies can do without
many changes of clothes. At the most pack 2 outfits
per day. Pack mix and match type clothes for your
little one as well. Pick things which are comfortable
to wear and quick to dry.

36. SELECTING SHOES FOR YOUR BABY

Like outfits, kids can make do with two pairs of
comfortable shoes. If you can get some water
resistant shoes it will be best. To expedite drying wet
shoes, you can stuff newspaper in them then wrap

them with newspaper and leave them to dry
overnight.

37. KEEP ONE CHANGE OF CLOTHES HANDY

Travelling with kids can be tricky. Keep a change of
clothes for the kids and mum handy in your purse or
tote bag. This takes a bit of space in your hand
luggage but comes extremely handy in case there are
any accidents or spills.

38. LEAVE BEHIND BABY ACCESSORIES

Baby accessories like their bed, bath tub, car seat, crib
etc. should be left at home. Many hotels provide a
crib on request, while car seats can be borrowed from
friends or rented. Babies can be given a bath in the
hotel sink or even in the adult bath tub with a little bit
of water. If you bring a few bath toys, they can be
used in the bath, pool, and out of water. They can also
be sanitized easily in the sink.

39. CARRY A SMALL LOAD OF PLASTIC BAGS

With children around there are chances of a number
of soiled clothes and diapers. These plastic bags help
to sort the dirt from the clean inside your big bag.

These are very light weight and come in handy to other carry stuff as well at times.

PACK WITH A PURPOSE

40. PACKING FOR BUSINESS TRIPS

One neutral-colored suit should suffice. It can be paired with different shirts, ties and accessories for different occasions. One pair of black suit pants could be worn with a matching jacket for the office or with a snazzy top for dinner.

41. PACKING FOR A CRUISE

Most cruises have formal dinners, and that formal dress usually takes up a lot of space. However you might find a tuxedo to rent. For women, a short black dress with multiple accessory options will do the trick.

42. PACKING FOR A LONG TRIP OVER DIFFERENT CLIMATES

The secret packing mantra for travel over multiple climates is layering. Layering traps air around your body creating insulation against the cold. The same light t-shirt that is comfortable in a warmer climate can be the innermost layer in a colder climate.

REDUCE SOME MORE WEIGHT

43. LEAVE PRECIOUS THINGS AT HOME

Things that you would hate to lose or get damaged leave them at home. Precious jewelry, expensive gadgets or dresses, could be anything. You will not require these on your trip. Leave them at home and spare the load on your mind.

44. SEND SOUVENIRS BY MAIL

If you have spent all your money on purchasing souvenirs, carrying them back in the same bag that you brought along would be difficult. Either pack everything in another bag and check it in the airport or get everything shipped to your home. Use an international carrier for a secure transit, but this could be more expensive than the checking fees at the airport.

45. AVOID CARRYING BOOKS

Books equal to weight. There are many reading apps which you can download on your smart phone or tab.

Plus there are gadgets like Kindle and Nook that are thinner and lighter alternatives to your regular book.

CHECK, GET, SET, CHECK AGAIN

46. STRATEGIZE BEFORE PACKING

Create a travel list and prepare all that you think you need to carry along. Keep everything on your bed or floor before packing and then think through once again – do I really need that? Any item that meets this question can be avoided. Remove whatever you don't really need and pack the rest.

47. TEST YOUR LUGGAGE

Once you have fully packed for the trip take a test trip with your luggage. Take your bags and go to town for window shopping for an hour. If you enjoy your hour long trip it is good to go, if not, go home and reduce the load some more. Repeat this test till you hit the right weight.

48. ADD A ROLL OF DUCT TAPE

You might wonder why, when this book has been talking about reducing stuff, we're suddenly asking you to pack something totally unusual. This is because when you have limited supplies, duct tape is immensely helpful for small repairs – a broken bag, leaking zip-lock bag, broken sunglasses, you name it and duct tape can fix it, temporarily.

49. LIST OF ESSENTIAL ITEMS

Even though the emphasis is on packing light, there are things which have to be carried for any trip. Here is our list of essentials:

• Passport/Visa or any other ID

• Any other paper work that might be required on a trip like permits, hotel reservation confirmations etc.

• Medicines – all your prescription medicines and emergency kit, especially if you are travelling with children

• Medical or vaccination records

• Money in foreign currency if travelling to a different country

• Tickets- Email or Message them to your phone

50. MAKE THE MOST OF YOUR TRIP

Wherever you are going, whatever you hope to do we encourage you to embrace it whole-heartedly. Take in the scenery, the culture and above all, enjoy your time away from home.

On a long journey even a straw weighs heavy.

-Spanish Proverb

PACKING AND PLANNING TIPS

A Week before Leaving

- Arrange for someone to take care of pets and water plants.

- Stop mail and newspaper.

- Notify Credit Card companies where you are going.

- Change your thermostat settings.

- Car inspected, oil is changed, and tires have the correct pressure.

- Passports and photo identification is up to date.

- Pay bills.

- Copy important items and download travel Apps.

- Start collecting small bills for tips.

Right Before Leaving

- Clean out refrigerator.

- Empty garbage cans.

- Lock windows.

- Make sure you have the proper identification with you.

- Bring cash for tips.

- Remember travel documents.

- Lock door behind you.

- Remember wallet.

- Unplug items in house and pack chargers.

>TOURIST

READ OTHER
GREATER THAN A TOURIST
BOOKS

Greater Than a Tourist San Miguel de Allende Guanajuato Mexico:
50 Travel Tips from a Local by Tom Peterson

Greater Than a Tourist – Lake George Area New York USA:
50 Travel Tips from a Local by Janine Hirschklau

Greater Than a Tourist – Monterey California United States:
50 Travel Tips from a Local by Katie Begley

Greater Than a Tourist – Chanai Crete Greece:
50 Travel Tips from a Local by Dimitra Papagrigoraki

Greater Than a Tourist – The Garden Route Western Cape Province
South Africa: 50 Travel Tips from a Local by Li-Anne McGregor van
Aardt

Greater Than a Tourist – Sevilla Andalusia Spain:
50 Travel Tips from a Local by Gabi Gazon

Greater Than a Tourist – Kota Bharu Kelantan Malaysia:
50 Travel Tips from a Local by Aditi Shukla

Children's Book: Charlie the Cavalier Travels the World by Lisa
Rusczyk

> TOURIST

Visit Greater Than a Tourist for Free Travel Tips
http://GreaterThanATourist.com

Sign up for the Greater Than a Tourist Newsletter for discount days, new books, and travel information:
http://eepurl.com/cxspyf

Follow us on Facebook for tips, images, and ideas:
https://www.facebook.com/GreaterThanATourist

Follow us on Pinterest for travel tips and ideas:
http://pinterest.com/GreaterThanATourist

Follow us on Instagram for beautiful travel images:
http://Instagram.com/GreaterThanATourist

> TOURIST

Please leave your honest review of this book on Amazon and Goodreads. Please send your feedback to GreaterThanaTourist@gmail.com as we continue to improve the series. We appreciate your positive and constructive feedback. Thank you.

METRIC CONVERSIONS

TEMPERATURE

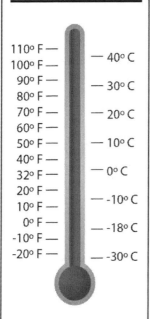

110° F —	— 40° C
100° F —	
90° F —	— 30° C
80° F —	
70° F —	— 20° C
60° F —	
50° F —	— 10° C
40° F —	
32° F —	— 0° C
20° F —	
10° F —	— -10° C
0° F —	
-10° F —	— -18° C
-20° F —	— -30° C

To convert F to C:

Subtract 32, and then multiply by 5/9 or .5555.

To Convert C to F:

Multiply by 1.8 and then add 32.

32F = 0C

LIQUID VOLUME

To Convert:...................Multiply by
U.S. Gallons to Liters................ 3.8
U.S. Liters to Gallons 26
Imperial Gallons to U.S. Gallons 1.2
Imperial Gallons to Liters....... 4.55
Liters to Imperial Gallons 22
1 Liter = .26 U.S. Gallon
1 U.S. Gallon = 3.8 Liters

DISTANCE

To convert ....Multiply by
Inches to Centimeters 2.54
Centimeters to Inches 39
Feet to Meters....................... .3
Meters to Feet 3.28
Yards to Meters 91
Meters to Yards 1.09
Miles to Kilometers 1.61
Kilometers to Miles............ .62
1 Mile = 1.6 km
1 km = .62 Miles

WEIGHT

1 Ounce = .28 Grams
1 Pound = .4555 Kilograms
1 Gram = .04 Ounce
1 Kilogram = 2.2 Pounds

TRAVEL QUESTIONS

- Do you bring presents home to family or friends after a vacation?

- Do you get motion sick?

- Do you have a favorite billboard?

- Do you know what to do if there is a flat tire?

- Do you like a sun roof open?

- Do you like to eat in the car?

- Do you like to wear sun glasses in the car?

- Do you like toppings on your ice cream?

- Do you use public bathrooms?

- Did you bring your cell phone and does it have power?

- Do you have a form of identification with you?

- Have you ever been pulled over by a cop?

- Have you ever given money to a stranger on a road trip?

- Have you ever taken a road trip with animals?

- Have you ever went on a vacation alone?

- Have you ever run out of gas?

- If you could move to any place in the world, where would it be?

- If you could travel anywhere in the world, where would you travel?

- If you could travel in any vehicle, which one would it be?

- If you had three things to wish for from a magic genie, what would they be?

- If you have a driver's license, how many times did it take you to pass the test?

- What are you the most afraid of on vacation?

- What do you want to get away from the most when you are on vacation?

- What foods smells bad to you?

- What item do you bring on ever trip with you away from home?

- What makes you sleepy?

- What song would you love to hear on the radio when you're cruising on the highway?

- What travel job would you want the least?

- What will you miss most while you are away from home?

- What is something you always wanted to try?

- What is the best road side attraction that you ever saw?

- What is the farthest distance you ever biked?

- What is the farthest distance you ever walked?

- What is the weirdest thing you needed to buy while on vacation?

- What is your favorite candy?

- What is your favorite color car?

- What is your favorite family vacation?

- What is your favorite food?

- What is your favorite gas station drink or food?

- What is your favorite license plate design?

- What is your favorite restaurant?

- What is your favorite smell?

- What is your favorite song?

- What is your favorite sound that nature makes?

- What is your favorite thing to bring home from a vacation?

- What is your favorite vacation with friends?

- What is your favorite way to relax?

- Where is the farthest place you ever traveled in a car?

- Where is the farthest place you ever went North, South, East and West?

- Where is your favorite place in the world?

- Who is your favorite singer?

- Who taught you how to drive?

- Who will you miss the most while you are away?

- Who if the first person you will contact when you get to your destination?

- Who brought you on your first vacation?

- Who likes to travel the most in your life?

- Would you rather be hot or cold?

- Would you rather drive above, below, or at the speed limited?

- Would you rather drive on a highway or a back road?

- Would you rather go on a train or a boat?

- Would you rather go to the beach or the woods?

TRAVEL BUCKET LIST

1.

2.

3.

4.

5.

6.

7.

8.

9.

10.

NOTES

Made in the USA
Monee, IL
23 December 2021

87037242R00065